DATE DUE

4			

DEMCO 38-297

Abraham Lincoln

Assassination of Abraham Lincoln

Cornerstones of Freedom

The Story of

FORD'S THEATER AND THE DEATH OF LINCOLN

By Zachary Kent

 CHILDRENS PRESS ®

CHICAGO

Lincoln died in
William Petersen's
boardinghouse
across the street from
Ford's Theater.

Library of Congress Cataloging-in-Publication Data

Kent, Zachary.
    The story of Ford's Theater and the death of Lincoln.

    (Cornerstones of freedom)
    Summary: Describes the events leading up to the
assassination of Abraham Lincoln, the conspiracy
involved in that slaying, and the aftermath of the
tragic event.
    1.   Lincoln, Abraham, 1809-1865—Assassination—
Juvenile literature. [1. Lincoln, Abraham, 1809-1865—
Assassination] I. Title. II. Series.
E457.5.K43   1987   973.7'092'4   87-17662
ISBN 0-516-04729-9

Childrens Press®, Chicago
Copyright © 1987 by Regensteiner Publishing Enterprises, Inc.
All rights reserved. Published simultaneously in Canada.
Printed in the United States of America.
    4 5 6 7 8 9 10 R 96 95 94 93 92 91 90

Late on the night of April 14, 1865, a stunned audience surged out of Ford's Theater and into the darkened Washington, D.C., street. "Abraham Lincoln has been shot!" some shouted. "President Lincoln is dying!" yelled others, running to spread the awful news. Men and women stood together, weeping, confused, and frightened. Alerted by the noise, people from neighboring houses soon joined the swirling mass on Tenth Street.

Through the theater doorway a cluster of soldiers appeared. "Out of the way!" roared a captain. "Clear out! Clear out!" Thrusting his sword left and right, the officer forced an opening through the crowd. Pressing close on every side, shocked bystanders watched the soldiers slowly carry the limp and bloodied president in their arms across the street.

"Get him to the White House!" demanded a concerned voice.

The doctor supporting Lincoln's head in his hands refused. "He would die on the way," he warned.

"Bring him in here!" shouted a man holding a lighted candle.

Carefully the soldiers climbed the steps of

The room where Lincoln died

William Petersen's boardinghouse. In a small room at the far end of the hall they laid the wounded man on a bed. There was no hope for President Lincoln. The bullet was lodged in his brain. As word blazed across the city and hummed over telegraph wires, Americans shook with sadness. During a time of national triumph, an assassin's single bullet plunged the nation into the deepest despair.

Since 1861 the United States had been gripped in bloody civil war. A long raging argument over slavery had torn the country in two. In the North where factories thrived, thousands of European immigrants were willing to work long hours for low wages. Most Northerners had no use for slavery and many considered it to be cruel and immoral. The South, however, depended upon slavery for the success of its farming economy.

The 1860 election of Abraham Lincoln as sixteenth president of the United States brought the problem to its final crisis. Many angry Southerners feared that Lincoln, a Northerner from Illinois, planned to abolish slavery. Rather than submit, eleven Southern states quit the Union and formed the Confederate States of America with Jefferson Davis as their president.

In April 1861, Confederate soldiers bombarded Fort Sumter in the harbor of Charleston, South

Soldiers looking out across the harbor at Fort Sumter

Painting done in 1888 of the Battle of Antietam

Carolina, forcing the withdrawal of the Union garrison. The next day Lincoln called upon loyal troops to put down the rebellion. Soon the land shook with the crack of musketfire and the crash of thundering cannon. On a hundred battlefields with names like Bull Run, Shiloh, Antietam, Gettysburg, and Chickamauga stubborn blue-clad Union soldiers and tough Confederates dressed in gray fiercely clashed until more than 600,000 Americans lay buried in the ground. Saddened by the bloodshed, still Lincoln remained determined to hold the nation together, and through four long years Northerners rallied around him.

At last, during the first two weeks of April 1865, the people of Washington, D.C., experienced excitement day after day. On April 4 men and boys rushed along Pennsylvania Avenue shouting, "Richmond has fallen! Richmond has fallen!" Union soldiers had captured the Confederate capital. Then on April 9 even more wonderful news reached Washington. Confederate General Robert E. Lee had surrendered his army to Union General Ulysses S. Grant at the Virginia village of Appomattox Court House.

As the word spread, people cheered in the streets and strangers hugged one another. City church bells loudly rang, and on the Potomac River steamboat whistles blew. Business stopped completely as all of Washington wildly celebrated. On the night of April 11 grateful citizens gathered on the White House lawn and chanted, "Lincoln! Lincoln!"

With final victory in sight, Lincoln stepped to a window and talked to this crowd. In his second inaugural address the previous March he had proclaimed: "With malice toward none; with charity for all . . . let us strive on to finish the work we are in; to bind up the nation's wounds." Now the fifty-six-year-old president spoke again of his desire to reunite the country quickly.

His speech finished, Lincoln joined his wife, Mary, and some friends in the Red Room of the White House. As they sipped tea, Mrs. Lincoln noticed how solemn her husband looked. She asked him what bothered him, and Lincoln talked about a recent dream.

"About ten days ago," he said, "I retired very late. . . . I could not have been long in bed when I fell into a slumber, for I was weary. I soon began to dream. There seemed to be a deathlike stillness about me. Then I heard subdued sobs, as if a number of people were weeping. I thought I left my bed and wandered downstairs.

". . . I was puzzled and alarmed. What could be the meaning of all this? Determined to find the cause . . . I kept on until I arrived in the East Room, which I entered. There I met with a sickening surprise. Before me was a catafalque [an elaborate funeral platform] on which rested a corpse. . . . Around it were stationed soldiers . . . and there was a throng of people, some gazing mournfully upon the corpse . . . others weeping pitifully.

" 'Who is dead in the White House?' I demanded of one of the soldiers.

" 'The President,' was his answer. 'He was killed by an assassin.'

"Then came a loud burst of grief from the crowd, which awoke me from my dream."

"That is horrid," exclaimed Mrs. Lincoln.

"It was only a dream, Mother," said the president. "Let us say no more about it, and try to forget it."

In truth, Lincoln had every reason to worry about his life. Bitter Southerners blamed him for the war and all their misery. The target of deep hatred since taking office, Lincoln kept a big envelope labeled "Assassination" in his desk. Crammed inside were eighty different letters containing murder threats against him.

Yet the president remained unafraid. "What does anybody want to assassinate me for?" he asked his friend, Ward Hill Lamon. "If anyone wants to do so, he can do it any day or night, if he is ready to give his life for mine. It is nonsense." Although he did not want special protection, starting in 1865 four city

Lincoln was warned several times about threats to his life.

policemen worked shifts as his bodyguard, and many nights Federal Marshal Lamon walked the hall outside of Lincoln's bedroom.

The people of Washington, D.C., greeted the morning of April 14, 1865, Good Friday, with feelings of peace and hope. At the White House, the president sat comfortably at his desk and conducted interviews with the congressmen, government officials, and private citizens who filed into his office with requests. Shortly after ten o'clock he remembered an errand and sent a messenger to Ford's Theater on Tenth Street. Mrs. Lincoln wanted to attend the theater that night, and Lincoln asked that a box be reserved for them. He hoped to bring General Grant and Mrs. Grant along as his guests.

"I have never felt so happy in my life," Lincoln told his wife during a pleasant carriage ride that afternoon. Later, however, darker notions again entered the president's mind. While walking with his daytime bodyguard, William H. Crook, he said, "Crook, do you know, I believe there are men who want to take my life?—And I have no doubt they will do it."

Of his wife's theater plan, he mentioned: "It has been advertised that we will be there and I cannot disappoint the people. Otherwise, I would not go," adding quietly, "— I do not want to go."

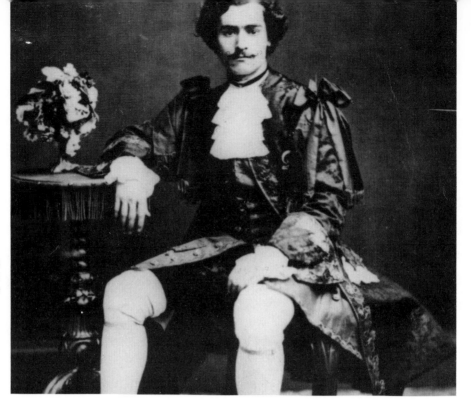

President Lincoln's misgivings and strange feelings of danger would soon prove themselves well-founded. Even as he spoke, one man, John Wilkes Booth, plotted to murder him. Twenty-six years old and handsome with dark eyes and jet black hair and moustache, Booth was a popular stage actor from a famous family of actors.

Born in the border state of Maryland, Booth identified with the South. Secretly he wished to make himself famous by doing something to help the noble Confederate cause. In 1864 he remarked, "What a glorious opportunity there is for a man to immortalize himself by killing Lincoln." Drawing an odd group of admirers about him, during the next year

Booth planned to kidnap President Lincoln. Meeting at Mrs. Mary Surratt's H Street boardinghouse, Booth, Michael O'Laughlin, Samuel Arnold, George Atzerodt, David Herold, John Surratt, and later a brawny young man named Lewis Paine, agreed on kidnapping plans but failed twice to carry them out. As the civil war rushed to a finish in April 1865, Booth madly vowed to kill the president at the very first opportunity.

When staying in Washington, Booth used Ford's Theater as his mailing address. At noon on April 14 he walked into the great brick building to pick up his letters and learned President Lincoln expected to attend the theater that evening. Hiding his excitement, Booth asked a few questions and then left. His chance to assassinate Lincoln finally had arrived.

John T. Ford owned Ford's Theater, but during his absence that day his brothers, James and Harry, prepared for the president's visit. Stagehands removed the partition separating boxes seven and eight, and carried comfortable sofas, chairs, and a red upholstered rocker into the joined boxes. Across the front of the boxes Harry Ford draped American banners, hung a Treasury Guards flag, and nailed a framed portrait of George Washington. Standing on the stage, the men admired these decorations and then went about their other business.

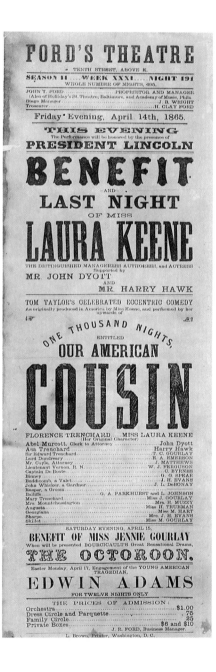

Ford's Theater (above) as it looks today. A poster (right) announcing the play that the Lincolns attended

No one knows exactly when, but sometime in the late afternoon John Wilkes Booth sneaked back into Ford's Theater and examined the president's box. Then he made secret preparations of his own. Hurrying about the city afterwards, he rented a horse, issued instructions to his remaining three plotters, Paine, Herold, and Atzerodt, and ate dinner at the National Hotel. Later he chatted with the hotel desk clerk and suggested the man attend Ford's Theater. "You will see some fine acting tonight," he promised with a smile.

The crowd of seventeen hundred people who filled Ford's Theater that night certainly expected a carefree time. The play that evening was *Our American Cousin,* a comedy about a simple Yankee

The President's Box was to the right of the stage.

who attempts to inherit the fortune of his noble English relatives. The show was well under way when at 8:25 P.M. the president's carriage arrived. General Grant and his wife had turned down their theater invitations. Instead, a young War Department attaché, Major Henry Reed Rathbone and his fiancée, Miss Clara Harris, the daughter of New York Senator Ira Harris, joined President and Mrs. Lincoln as their guests.

Lincoln's nighttime bodyguard, John F. Parker, escorted them from the theater lobby upstairs to their box. Although instructed to sit outside the door, before long Parker thoughtlessly left his post and took a seat in the balcony so he could watch the play. Sometime afterward, he walked out of the theater altogether.

Upon the arrival of the presidential party, the performance stopped. Loud applause greeted President Lincoln, and the orchestra played "Hail to the Chief." Soon everyone resumed their seats and the play continued. One young woman, Julia Shephard, impressed by the event, wrote a quick note to her father back home: "The President is in yonder upper right hand private box so handsomely decked with silken flags festooned over a picture of George Washington. The young and lovely daughter of Senator Harris is the only one of the party we can see, as the flags hide the rest. But we know 'Father Abraham' is there, like a father watching what interests his children. . . . How sociable it seems, like one family sitting around their parlor fire . . ."

In lighthearted spirits, Mrs. Lincoln, Major Rathbone, and Miss Harris laughed at every joke in the play. Slouching in the upholstered rocker, however, President Lincoln often seemed preoccupied. Fondly Mary Lincoln pressed close to her husband, and soon she whispered, "What will Miss Harris think of my hanging on to you so?" The President answered quietly, "She won't think anything about it."

Those were to be his final words.

At about nine-thirty, John Wilkes Booth trotted his rented mare into the alley behind Ford's Theater. He called out several times until a young theater worker stepped up to hold the horse for him. Then he entered the rear of the theater and used a special passageway to cross under the stage. Making his way through to a side alley door, he walked around to Tenth Street.

During the next half hour Booth nervously paced in and out of the theater lobby several times. He drank whiskey at the neighboring Star Saloon and chatted with the bartender. Shortly after ten o'clock he entered the Ford's Theater lobby once more.

Approaching the ticket-taker, the well-known actor joked, "You will not want a ticket from me?" and freely passed inside.

The assassin gazed at the main floor audience and at the actors on stage. Then he climbed the winding staircase that led to the lower balcony. Surprised to find no guard, he slipped into the narrow passage that led to the president's box. Inside, he turned and closed the passage door. In the dark he found a short length of wood he had left there in the afternoon. He wedged this stake against the door so no one else could enter the passage. Earlier he also had carved a peephole in the door that led into the president's box. Now he groped forward and put his eye to it. Beyond, he saw the rocking chair and the outline of the president's head.

The performance was reaching the end of the second scene of Act III. Harry Hawk, in the role of the American cousin, Asa Trenchard, stood alone on stage delivering his final lines. "Don't know the manner of good society, eh? Well, I guess I know enough to turn you inside out, old gal — you sock-dologizing old mantrap!"

Timing his movement carefully Booth opened the box door and drew a derringer pistol from his pocket. As the audience roared with laughter, he stepped forward, aimed, and pulled the trigger. At

close range the bullet struck Lincoln behind the left
ear and smashed deep within his skull. The impact
tilted him forward a bit in his chair, and then he
slumped back.

Gunsmoke clouded the air as Mary Lincoln and
Clara Harris stared at Booth in shocked confusion.
Major Rathbone jumped up and tried to grapple
with the murderer. Quickly Booth dropped the derringer and pulled out a hunting knife. Lunging
wildly, he slashed Rathbone across the upper left
arm. Then he climbed over the railing of the box.
Vaulting to the stage twelve feet below, the spur on
his right boot caught in the Treasury flag. The ban-

ner ripped and Booth landed awkwardly, breaking his left leg above the ankle. Striking a pose before the surprised audience the crazed actor shouted, "Sic Semper Tyrannis!" the Latin motto of Virginia, meaning "Thus always with tyrants!"

"Stop that man!" shouted Major Rathbone.

The audience stood. In panic, people filled the aisles. What had happened? they wondered. Completely stunned, they heard Major Rathbone call out: "He has shot the President!"

Limping hurriedly away, the assassin found his way to the back alley, leaped onto his horse, and galloped off into the night.

"Water!" begged Miss Harris.

"Help! Help!" shrieked Mrs. Lincoln.

Soon men pounded on the passage door leading to the president's box. His wounded arm dripping blood, Major Rathbone discovered and removed the wooden brace. Opening the door, he pleaded that only doctors be admitted. Charles Leale, a young army surgeon, pushed through the mob. In moments he reached the president's side.

"Oh, Doctor! Is he dead?" moaned Mary Lincoln. "Can he recover? Will you take charge of him? Oh, my dear husband!"

"I will do what I can," Leale told her. Quickly he examined the president and found him unconscious and barely breathing. A lamp was brought and men helped lay him on the floor. With a pocket knife, Leale slit the president's shirt and collar but discovered no injury. Running his fingers through the dying man's hair, at last he found the bloody wound. Bent over his patient, Leale attempted artificial respiration. As other doctors arrived in the box, however, he sadly stated his opinion: "His wound is mortal. It is impossible for him to recover."

Men and women in the crowded passageway began to weep. Laura Keene, the leading lady of *Our American Cousin*, found her way into the box and asked to cradle the president's head in her lap and bathe it with water. In a few moments Leale and his fellow doctors decided Lincoln should be moved to a bed somewhere nearby. Four artillerymen stepped forward to carry the body. Holding the president's head, Dr. Leale yelled, "Guards! Guards! Clear the passage!"

Down the theater stairs, past dazed and tearful onlookers, the men carefully moved ahead. As they crossed muddy Tenth Street, Henry Safford, a tenant at Petersen's boardinghouse, motioned them inside. The soldiers stepped gently up the stairs with their burden and into the three-story brick building.

"Take me to your best room!" commanded Dr. Leale.

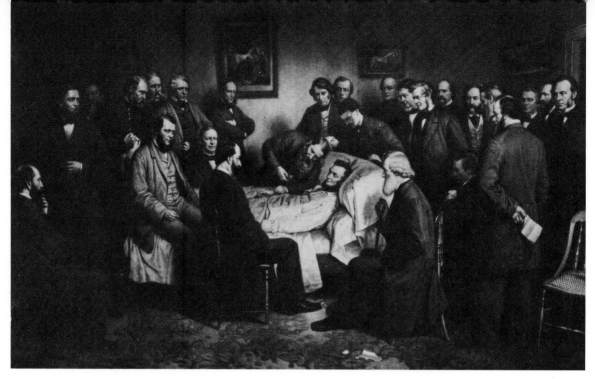

Members of Lincoln's cabinet gathered around the dying Lincoln.

Safford led the group to the room of army private William T. Clark at the rear of the house. At last they placed Lincoln on a low bed with clean sheets. To make a more complete examination, Dr. Leale and his fellow physicians removed the president's clothes, starting with his long frock coat and his giant size-fourteen boots. To fit the six-foot-four-inch president more comfortably, they laid him diagonally across the cornhusk mattress and propped his head upon pillows. Soldiers hurried along the narrow hallway hopelessly bringing hot water bottles, mustard plasters, and blankets. Through the night cabinet members, congressmen, friends of Lincoln, Ford's Theater actors, and complete strangers entered the house, walked the hall, and crowded into the little room. Crying and praying, they all wanted a last glimpse of the dying president.

Seated in the front parlor, Mary Lincoln was hysterical. "Why did he not shoot me instead of my husband?" she wailed. "I have tried to be so careful of him. . . . How can it be so!" Tearfully, twenty-one-year-old Robert Lincoln tried to comfort his mother.

In another sitting room, Secretary of War Edwin Stanton took control and launched an investigation of the affair. The plot, he knew, extended beyond the attack on President Lincoln. At about 10:15 that night a stranger—Lewis Paine—had forced his way into Secretary of State William Seward's house. Badly hurt in a carriage accident nine days before, Seward lay helpless in his bedroom. After attacking family members, Paine slashed at the secretary with a knife, and then ran away. Only the metal brace supporting Seward's previously broken jaw and shoulder saved the injured man's life. As another part of Booth's insane plan to avenge the fallen South, George Atzerodt was to murder Vice-President Andrew Johnson that night as well. But Atzerodt lost his nerve and got drunk instead. Into the rainy morning hours Stanton gathered information on these crimes, alerted army patrols, and ordered speedy arrests.

At Lincoln's bedside, the doctors attempted to locate and remove the bullet. Twice, Surgeon General Joseph Barnes inserted long metal probes into the wound, but he failed to draw out the bullet. After seven o'clock the president's breathing grew more shallow. His skin turned icy cold to the touch. Secretary of the Navy Gideon Welles remembered: "His wife soon after made her last visit to him. The death-struggle had begun. Robert, his son, stood with several others at the head of the bed. He bore himself well, but on two occasions gave way to over-powering grief and sobbed aloud." Unable to bear the scene, Mary Lincoln moaned and fled the room.

At 7:22 A.M., April 15, 1865, Abraham Lincoln died. John Hay, the president's personal secretary, observed that "a look of unspeakable peace came over his worn features." The men in the room stood with bowed heads, and Secretary Stanton sadly uttered: "Now he belongs to the ages."

Clicking telegraph keys swiftly spread the news of Lincoln's assassination. Newspapers edged with black headlined the shocking story. Church bells tolled in city and town, and mournful citizens hung black crepe on their doors and in their windows. With deep bitterness Northerners blamed the entire South for the bloody murder and demanded harsh revenge. Though the war was over, it would be generations before its wounds were healed completely.

Secretary of War Stanton saw that the Lincoln conspirators were brought quickly to justice. Great rewards were offered, and soldiers tracked down John Wilkes Booth. Cornered in a tobacco barn near Bowling Green, Virginia, on April 25, Booth refused to surrender. Soldiers set fire to the barn, and as Booth hopped around inside on crutches, Sergeant Boston Corbett spied him through a crack and shot him in the neck. Within a few hours Lincoln's killer died, mumbling the words, "Useless. Useless."

Apprehending John W. Booth on April 25

Reward poster issued
by the War
Department for the
capture of Lincoln's
assassins

In May, Washington citizens jammed a courtroom to watch the military trial of eight other suspected plotters. Four of them, Samuel Arnold, Michael O'Laughlin, Edward Spangler (a Ford's Theater stagehand), and Samuel Mudd (the Maryland doctor who set Booth's broken leg), received prison terms. The court condemned the other four: David Herold, Lewis Paine, George Atzerodt, and Mary Surratt. On July 7, hangmen fixed nooses around their necks, released the spring trapdoors, and watched them drop to their deaths.

Of the nine people involved in Lincoln's assassination (left), four were hanged (below).

Photograph of Lincoln's funeral as it moved slowly down Pennsylvania Avenue

Earlier, Northerners mourned the death of their martyred president in much more elaborate ceremonies. In the East Room of the White House carpenters hammered together a platform with an arched canopy. On this catafalque Lincoln's coffin rested, just as it had been predicted in his dream. Two days later a great procession of soldiers and mourners followed the horse-drawn hearse that carried the body to the Capitol rotunda where the president lay in state. On April 21 an honor guard placed the coffin aboard a special train. Rattling slowly northward, the train carried Lincoln on his final journey home to Springfield, Illinois.

Just four years earlier Lincoln had left that city bound for his first presidential inauguration. The nation stood on the brink of civil war on that rainy February 11, 1861, and in a touching farewell speech Lincoln told the gathered crowd, "To this place, and the kindness of these people, I owe everything. . . . I now leave, not knowing when, or whether ever, I may return, with a task before me greater than that which rested upon Washington."

On May 3, 1865, old friends saw the president's coffin entombed among the shady trees at Springfield's Oak Ridge Cemetery. Abraham Lincoln's life and labors were done, and the Union was preserved.

Thousands of people gathered at Oak Ridge Cemetery.

From Washington, D.C. a train carried President Lincoln's body
home to Springfield, Illinois.

About the Author

   Zachary Kent grew up in Little Falls, New Jersey, and received an English degree
from St. Lawrence University. Following college he worked at a New York City liter-
ary agency for two years and then launched his writing career. To support himself
while writing, he has worked as a taxi driver, a shipping clerk, and a house painter.
Mr. Kent has had a lifelong interest in American history. Studying the U.S. presidents
was his childhood hobby. His collection of presidential items includes books, pictures,
and games, as well as several autographed letters.